Strange ... But True?

THE BERMUDA TRIANGLE

ELIZABETH NOLL

BLACK
RABBIT
BOOKS

Bolt is published by Black Rabbit Books
P.O. Box 3263, Mankato, Minnesota, 56002.
www.blackrabbitbooks.com
Copyright © 2017 Black Rabbit Books

Design and Production by Michael Sellner
Photo Research by Rhonda Milbrett

Library of Congress Control Number: 2015954863

HC ISBN: 978-1-68072-021-1   PB ISBN: 978-1-68072-291-8

Printed in the United States at CG Book Printers,
North Mankato, Minnesota, 56003. 2/18

BOLT

Image Credits
Adobe Stock: Nomad_Soul, 1;
Corbis: adoc-photos, Cover; Dream-
stime: breakermaximus, 20; Philcold, 18-
19; fanshare.com: 15 (front); ghosthuntingth-
eories.com: 23; iStock: Owen Price, 18 (compass);
Pobytov, 3, 11, 32; Newscom: ITV/REX, 4-5; pxleyes.
com: anjo1989, 24–25; Shutterstock: Andrey VP, 17;
Anton Balazh, 8-9; Christos Georghiou, 31; cobalt88,
16; die Fotosynthese, 6; Linda Bucklin, 15 (back);
Mr Doomits, 22-23; Robert Kneschke, 17 (arrow);
Seamartini Graphics, 28; Superstock: Steve Bloom
Images, 12; therichest.com: 26
Every effort has been made to contact copyright
holders for material reproduced in this
book. Any omissions will be rectified in
subsequent printings if notice is
given to the publisher.

Contents

Five planes flew over the ocean. The pilots thought they were near the Bermuda Triangle. But they didn't recognize the islands below. One pilot called for help. "We seem to be off course."

Someone in the **control tower** told the pilots to fly west. But the pilots' **compasses** didn't work. The pilots flew one way. Then they flew another way. Then they just disappeared.

Nobody ever found the five planes. What happened to them? Some people **blame** the Bermuda Triangle. They say something there causes ships and planes to disappear.

Florida

Bermuda

BERMUDA TRIANGLE

Puerto
Rico

CHAPTER 2

Bermuda Triangle

The Bermuda Triangle's strange history is very old. Christopher Columbus wrote about lights there in 1492.

A U.S. Navy ship disappeared in the Bermuda Triangle in March 1918. The ship was carrying more than 300 people.

About 41 percent of people believe there's danger in the Bermuda Triangle.

BELIEVERS

41%

percent 0   10   20   30

Author Vincent Gaddis came up with the name "Bermuda Triangle." In 1965, he wrote a book about it. He said many ships and planes had **vanished** there. People began to believe it was a dangerous place.

Believers say more disappearances happen in the Triangle than anywhere else. They don't think most of the disappearances can be **explained** with science.

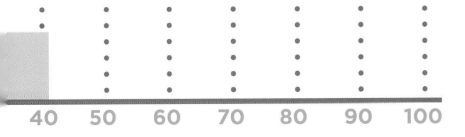

40   50   60   70   80   90   100

CHAPTER 3

Explaining the Bermuda Triangle

What could make ships and planes vanish? Some people think aliens mix up compasses. Then pilots get lost.

Other people think an old city is the trouble. Atlantis may have been a city that sank to the ocean floor. Maybe the sunken city has special powers.

Some stories tell of sea monsters that swallow ships. Maybe a monster lives in the Triangle.

Some people think there is a scientific explanation. Earth's **magnetic field** makes compasses point away from true north. Compasses pointing the wrong way could get people lost.

TRUE NORTH

N

MAGNETIC NORTH

S

MANY HURRICANES

WHAT'S GOING ON?

SPINNING
COMPASSES

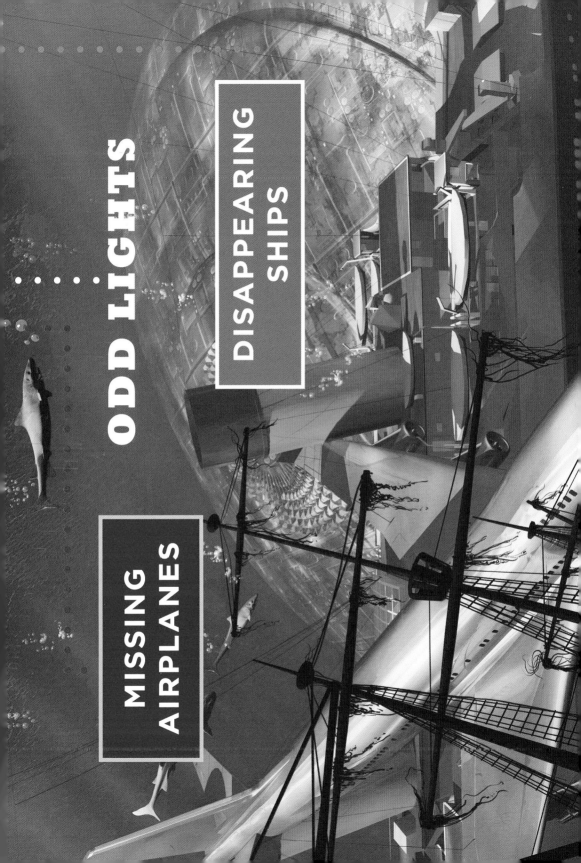

CHAPTER 4

Searching for Answers

Larry Kusche didn't believe the stories about the Triangle. In 1972, he began to study it. Kusche learned many of the stories were wrong. Many of the missing ships hadn't sunk in the Triangle.

The U.S. Coast Guard keeps records on the Triangle. This group says the area doesn't have more accidents than other places.

Kusche discovered other mistakes. Many reports said ships had sunk in calm weather. But Kusche learned they sank in bad storms. He also learned other stories were made up.

COMPARE THE DATA

Could hurricanes cause disappearances?

COMPARE THE DATA

Planes and Ships that disappeared in the Triangle area   **14**

Hurricanes in the Triangle   **3**

DECADE 1940s

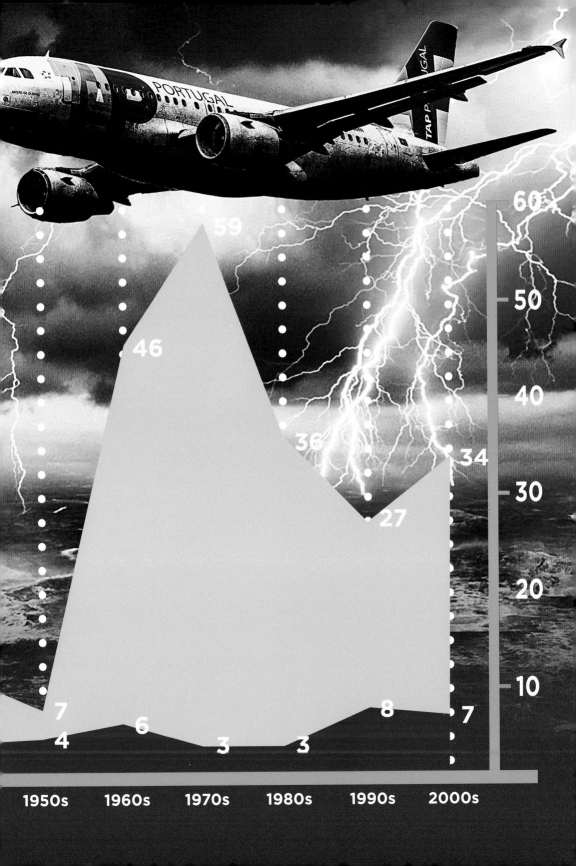

60

59

50

46

40

36

34

30

27

20

10

7
8
6
7
4
3
3

1950s   1960s   1970s   1980s   1990s   2000s

Some people think there are other places like the Bermuda Triangle. Some say Bridgewater Triangle in Massachusetts is mysterious. Others think a spot in Lake Michigan is too.

It's fun to think there's a place where aliens mix up compasses. But could there be simple answers behind the stories? You decide!

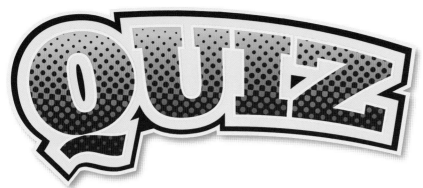

Believe It or Not?

Answer the questions below. Then add up your points to see if you believe.

1 **You hear of a ship that disappears. What do you think?**

A. There's no way the captain got lost! (3 points)

B. That's odd. You'd think today's tech could keep them on course. (2 points)

C. I'm sure the engine broke, and the ship sank. (1 point)

2 Do aliens or sea monsters exist?

A. definitely (3 points)

B. maybe (2 points)

C. not a chance (1 point)

3 Look at the graphs in this book again. What do you think?

A. The numbers don't lie. Something strange is going on. (3 points)

B. I'm not sure what to make of it. (2 points)

C. There's no mystery. (1 point)

. . . .

3 points:
There's no way you think something strange is happening.

4–8 points:
Maybe there is something going on. But then again, maybe not.

9 points:
You're a total believer!

blame (BLAYM)—to say or think that a person or thing is responsible for something bad that has happened

Coast Guard (KOST GARD)—a naval force that guards a coast or is responsible for the safety of ships in nearby waters

compass (KUM-pus)—a device used to find direction

control tower (kun-TROL TAH-wuhr)— a glass-enclosed structure where people direct the air and ground traffic at an airport

explain (EK-splayn)—to make something clear or easy to understand

magnetic field (mag-NE-tik FELD)—an area where an object's magnetic properties affect neighboring objects

vanish (VA-nish)—to disappear without explanation

30

BOOKS

Karst, Ken. *Bermuda Triangle*. Enduring Mysteries. Mankato, MN: Creative Education, 2015.

Lassieur, Allison. *Is the Bermuda Triangle Real?* Unexplained: What's the Evidence? Mankato, MN: Amicus, 2016.

McClellan, Ray. *The Bermuda Triangle*. Unexplained Mysteries. Minneapolis: Bellwether Media, Inc., 2014.

WEBSITES

Bermuda Triangle
www.history.com/topics/bermuda-triangle

The Truth Behind the Bermuda Triangle
channel.nationalgeographic.com/videos/bermuda-triangle-mystery/

INDEX